The Intentional Parent

PARENTING ON PURPOSE WHEN LIFE GETS BUSY

Susan Seay

A Powerful Moment Publishing

Austin, Texas

A Powerful Moment, LLC
PO Box 151355
Austin, Texas 78715
www.SusanSeay.com
Book Layout ©2013 BookDesignTemplates.com
Book Cover Design- MyAwesomeLogo.com

Ordering Information:
Quantity sales. Special discounts are available on quantity purchases by corporations, associations, and others. For details, contact the "Special Sales Department" at the address above.

The Intentional Parent/ Susan Seay—1st ed.
ISBN-13: 978-0692612118

Table of Contents

THE INTENTIONAL PARENT   1

THE HEART OF INTENTION   9

A BLESSING FOR YOU: 10

12 WAYS INTENTIONAL PARENTS ARE DIFFERENT   11

INTENTIONAL OR DISTRACTED?   17

LAY ASIDE EVERY WEIGHT   23

RELEASING THE WEIGHTS THAT HOLD US DOWN   27

THE EVER ELUSIVE SEARCH TO BE A 'GOOD MOM'   31

THE WEIGHT OF DECEPTION   37

THE WEIGHT OF COMPARISON   43

THE WEIGHT OF DISTRACTION   47

THE WEIGHT OF PUBLIC   OPINION   49

THE WEIGHT OF TOO MUCH INFORMATION   51

THE WEIGHT OF PERFECTION   53

RUN THE RACE WITH ENDURANCE   57

ASK BETTER QUESTIONS   59

UNDERSTAND RESPONSIBILITY   61

SET THE STANDARD   63

SPEAK THE TRUTH IN LOVE   67

REPHRASE THE PROBLEM   71

SEEKING EXPERT ADVICE   73

BUILDING A TEAM WORK ATTITUDE   75

THE STANDARD OF CAPABLE   79

OUR VOICE: THE POWER TO INFLUENCE   83

THE 4 EMOTIONS THAT PRECEDE ALL POOR
COMMUNICATION   89

CORE VALUES FOR THE FAMILY   93

UNDERSTANDING CORE VALUES   95

CASTING THE VISION WITH FAMILY VALUES   99

CHOOSING THE 'RIGHT' CORE VALUES   101

PUSHING THROUGH PROCRASTINATION   103

5 AREAS TO USE OUR CORE VALUES   105

I dedicate this book to my heavenly Father, my amazing and supportive husband, my children, family, and friends. This book never would have happened without each of you

Life is short.

Be intentional with every moment.

Susan Seay

---

10 Ways to Get the Most From This Book

1. Read the whole thing.

This book is small on purpose. There are no overly complex theories here, just simple steps you can use when life gets busy.

2. Pray through the book.

As you read along, ask God to reveal the truth of what it contains. Ask Him to show you new and creative ways to shift into intentional parenting.

3. Get messy!

When you find a certain phrase or question that really speaks to you, underline or highlight it. Each time you revisit the book, those sections will leap off the pages and serve as a reminder of key passages that had the most impact on you.

4. Use this book as a guide.

Remember this book is one small step in the journey to becoming more intentional. This is not the end, but a beautiful starting point. The mere fact that you are reading this book says that you're ready!

5. Share it with others.

We learn better when we teach. As you share the ideas in this book with others, you become better at applying these ideas in your own life. And you also will make it much more difficult to slip back into old habits that no longer serve you.

6. Resist the temptation to over-complicate things.

The methods shared within this book are simple by design. All too often we tend to complicate things and then fail because we can't keep up with the complicated plans we created. Let's give ourselves permission to simplify our busy lives.

7. Believe.

Believe in yourself. And have faith in God. It's no accident that this book is in your hands. This moment is an answer to my prayer that the right mom (and the right dad) would pick up this book and find answers to questions they didn't know to ask. If God could find a way to place this book into your hands, I ask that you also believe that He is actively at work to lead you every step of the way. As you read along, if you find yourself saying "I don't know", or if you genuinely feel lost or confused, turn your "I don't know" into a prayer request. Believe that God will answer you. For example- "I don't know what my core values are" turns into "Lord, I don't know what my core values are, can you reveal them to me?" Your answer will come in 1 of 3 ways.

1. God will reveal it to you,
2. He will bring the answer to you, or
3. He will lead you to the answer.

8. Do the work.

Just like being in a garage doesn't make you a car, owning a book on intentional parenting doesn't make you an intentional parent. Owning this book is a step that expresses the desire of your heart, but doing the work reveals your commitment to making it real. You don't need one more book to read. None of us do. But a book that can change your perspective and release you to rise to your true potential, that's a book you don't just read, it's a book you live! Do the work! Be an intentional parent!

9. Write to me and share your experiences.

I love to read success stories! Share your story with me. I can't wait to hear from you! Send your messages to Susan@SusanSeay.com

10. Intentional parenting is a calling.

Your desire to be an intentional parent is a God-given desire, and He is faithful to complete this work in you.

What good news!

Perhaps some part of you is scared that this book is going to be one more reminder of how you are failing as a parent. Maybe you secretly fear that as you read along you will be given a list of more things to do, and honestly, you already feel overwhelmed. Let me calm those fears. Nothing I have to share is meant to cause you to do anything but to pause and reflect. As you are reading, if you begin to feel anxious, worried, or doubtful, know that is not the Spirit of God. In Him you are promised joy, peace, patience, kindness, and more. If you become tempted to think that intentional parenting is all up to you, you will feel burdened. Remember that intentional parenting is a call from God and He will enable you to fulfill that call.

PROLOGUE

For all parents struggling to do the best for their family, yet still feel like it's never enough – this book is for us!

Everyone seems to have tons of advice for parents: how-to information, "well... when my kids were little" stories, and promises of the best tips to make your kids smarter and well behaved. But no matter how good the advice is, each of our families are unique.

Let's choose to be set free and grant each other permission to completely dismiss any and all parenting advice that doesn't fit our personality, our values, or the goals we have set for our family. This includes the ideas contained within this book. If it doesn't fit, release it. Otherwise, over time, we will find ourselves weighed down with burdens that rob us of the joy and strength we need to parent our children well.

This book was written to encourage all of us, including me the author, to be a parent on purpose. A parent who has clear core values for our family and uses those core values to set the standard for the daily details of family life. Parenting comes down to choosing between living with intention or living in reaction. It's a moment-by-moment choice.

With that in mind, this book is written for parents, both moms and dads. For ease of flow the word "mom" and the pronoun "she" will be used most often. I typically speak and teach to audiences full of moms. Whether stay-at-home moms, working moms, entrepreneurial moms, moms of many, or moms of just one, - it's usually a room full of moms. However, being an intentional parent applies to both moms and dads. Both parents will benefit from taking the time to ask themselves, "Am I being intentional with my family?"

I believe that God has not only charged us with a great responsibility as parents, but He has also given us the ability to raise the children He has placed in our care.

Together let's challenge our previously held beliefs about what is possible for each of our families. We just might be surprised to discover a fresh perspective awaiting us-- a perspective that releases our family to live life on purpose. Nothing missing. Holding nothing back.

Intentional parenting is the journey of a lifetime!

Parenting is hard work. There's no getting around that. I won't lie by saying that as a Mentor4Moms, I have the equivalent of an easy system for making our kids smart, well-behaved, and obedient. But what I do have to offer is a simple challenge- Rise above the noise and make the shift from distracted parenting to intentional. We each deserve to live a life that is on purpose and full of purpose.

Over the past nineteen years, so many moms have shared their heartfelt struggles with me. We have laughed and cried together. Sometimes we simply hugged and sat in silence. Those conversations left me with a deeper commitment to write a book that shares some of the encouragement and insights I have shared privately over the years. I now share these publicly to encourage moms I may never have the privilege of meeting face-to-face.

> *Rise above the noise and make the shift from distracted parenting to intentional.*

The Heart of Intention

At the end of our lives, we will reflect on what we have passed on to our children. Whether our house was clean or all the errands were run will mean nothing. However we will ask - What type of legacy did we leave? What types of values and character did we pass on to them? Have we done our best to prepare them for their future?

In this book, the goal is to raise our sense of purpose so that we passionately pursue intentional parenting. God didn't make a mistake when He chose us as parents. He wants us to look at our family and know that we were chosen for this work. It's a calling and privilege

A BLESSING FOR YOU:

May a deep and real sense of purpose fuel all your parenting efforts and cause you to become more intentional as a parent. May you become a parent who is able to rise above the noise and distractions that cry out for your attention every day. May you focus on living true to your core values. May you understand the importance of dedication and not allow other pursuits to drain your energy, leaving worn out. May your family always get the best of you, not just what's left of you.

12 Ways Intentional Parents Are Different

If we really want to become an intentional parent who successfully breaks free from the endless distractions and busy-ness that threatens to overwhelm us, we start by understanding the twelve things that intentional parents do differently.

Intentional parents aim to:

1. Make everyone in the family feel valuable and important, including mom. This starts with seeing mom as an irreplaceable person who is the heart of the home. When mom doesn't feel valued, the entire family suffers the loss of her whole-hearted contribution to the family.

2. Build strong family connections. Bonding with our family is part of being intentional. It's hard to be committed to people we don't know. When we allow busy-ness to pull the family away from one another in a bunch of different directions, it affects the family bond and weakens the sense of connection within the family.

11

3. Speak the truth in love. Even when it's scary or hard. Our voice as an intentional parent is so important to the lives of every person in our family. If we see trouble on the horizon, it's not loving to remain silent. If we see bad habits forming, wrong friendships, or laziness- speak up! Our voices stir our household to rise up to the best of who they are. Constantly encourage your family to shake off average thinking and rise to their full potential.

4. Admit when we're wrong. When we mess up, we fess up! No excuses, blaming, or hiding. We model for our kids what it looks like to take personal responsibility. We help them to see that it's okay to make mistakes. Personal responsibility sends the message that there's no need to hide our faults. When someone in the family makes a mistake, this is the process - we mess up, we fess up, we clean it up, and everyone moves on- together.

5. Build a teamwork attitude within the home. Our family is a unit, a team. We each depend on one another. Remind them often how much we need them. Build on the concept of team to foster unity and collaboration. Help everyone to feel a part of the team. We all can achieve more together than we could ever achieve apart.

6. Give each person lots of praise, and do it often. Positive attention, appreciation, and recognition go a long way in building confidence and self-esteem. Find things to praise in our kids. Take note of the character traits we see developing in them. Help them to see how much they've grown.

7. Delegate responsibility. Having a sense of responsibility and contribution helps everyone in the home to feel like they matter. Our children need to know that they are an important part of the family. Not only important, but needed. This distinction creates a sense of purpose and builds a sense of worth.

8. Believe in possibilities. If intentional parents are one thing, it's optimistic. They are full of hope about the future. They see great potential in themselves and their family. No matter the challenges or hardships they face, deep down, they believe better days are ahead.

9. Never stop learning. Intentional parents keep themselves keenly aware of the opportunities around them to better their best, expand their perspective, and shift from distracted to a place of purpose and intention. There are so many tools to help along the way, from the wise older neighbor, to the book in the library, the podcast or radio show, the conversation with a friend, or the observation of a family at the local park. Life is full of

opportunities to learn and grow and develop. Intentional parents understand that through learning and developing, they are able to stay in line with their purpose and live true to their core values.

10. Avoid the trap of perfectionism. Everyday as a parent, we have a lot of important decisions to make. As an intentional parent, we approach those decisions with a real sense of purpose and responsibility to our family. But if we become overly concerned with making the "right" decision, we may end up making no decision at all. Becoming overly concerned with making a mistake is in fact a mistake. Sometimes we will do our best, and it was not the right move. The attempt to always get it right will rob us of enjoying the journey. Don't buy into the myth of perfection.

11. Keep things simple. It's so much easier to be intentional with our family when we keep things simple. Over complicating things only leads to confusion. The moment things cease to be simple, we will begin to see our family lose interest and withdraw from the teamwork attitude we were trying to create.

12. Spend time with other parents who are also striving to be intentional. Find others who share the same focus of living on purpose in their homes. Families who seek to live life on purpose and with a deep sense of purpose.

Their expression of that purpose may look different than yours, but deep down, they are committed to being intentional and encouraging others to do the same. Finding these like-minded families will make the parenting journey sweet. Friends like this will become our go-to resources for ideas, encouragement, and support along the way.

Intentional or Distracted?

Before digging into the practical, let's start with defining the terms "distracted" and "intentional".

"Distracted" is when our attention is pulled away from a focus on what is most important. When we are not purposeful and taking deliberate action. Those times when we are going through the motions with no real sense of meaning or direction. And we consistently feel fear, doubt, worry, confusion, overwhelm, or a sense of hopelessness. The result of distracted parenting is always negative.

"Intentional" is when our attention is focused. We are clear on our purpose and deliberate in our actions. When we are intentional, we understand that all that we do in life is connected to our God-given purpose, and creates positive results.

The intentional parent and the distracted parent are on a continuum. On one end, there's intentional, and on the opposite end, there's distracted. At any given moment we can be completely focused and highly intentional, and the next moment we can be completely distracted. In fact, it's possible to go through this process so fast that it may seem like we're both at the same time.

An intentional parent versus a distracted parent is not Jane Doe versus Jill Doe. It's all Jane Doe. Both the intentional parent and the distracted parent are within all of us. The goal is to do our best to spend more time on the intentional side of the continuum, rising above the noise that pulls us towards distraction.

From time to time, our greatest desires for our family will run smack dab into reality. Our best intentions may not seem to be happening. It's at that moment we must decide whether to give into what we see or remain committed to our intention.

It's when things are really hard and seemingly out-of-control that our true intentions are revealed. We get to decide in that moment if what we want is really our deepest commitment to our family or if it was simply a good idea. If it's truly our deepest commitment, we will stick it out in spite of the circumstances and challenges. But if it's merely a good idea, then we will walk away.

For example, let's say our intention is to teach our kids to help out around the house. We teach them how to do a task. We ensure they understand how to complete it. Then we assign a few tasks to our children to complete. When we go back to check in, we find the work isn't done. After being reminded to complete the request they begin to whine or make excuses.

In that moment we have a choice.

We can slide to the distracted end of the continuum and focus only on their failure to do what we asked. After all, we asked them to do a task they are capable of handling and we gave them enough time.

OR

We can remain intentional in the moment.

Don't take it personally that they didn't follow through; instead, see it as a sign that there's more work to be done. It is possible to remain calm even when our children disappoint. None of us are calm 100% of the time. We all lose it from time to time, but it is easier to remain calm when we keep the bigger picture in mind.

Reacting is a sign that we are distracted. Reactions are charged with negative emotions while responses are deliberate and thoughtful. When we are intentional, we respond.

When we take the time to respond vs. react, we create more of what we want. Instead of reacting in a triggered, charged space, by blaming and making our children wrong, let's remember the closeness we desire in our family relationships. Lets be mindful to choose words that align with our commitment to move us toward one another and not further away.

Seize the daily moments to practice being intentional. After all, what if chore lists are not about the chores themselves, but the character traits our children develop along the way? Let's open our eyes to see the daily opportunities that are readily available to help us prepare our children for life. In time, we will be well on our way to not just having the occasional moment of intention, but adopting thoughtful, purpose-driven parenting as a lifestyle.

There is a direct connection between contribution and feeling valued. When our children contribute by working around the house they feel like a valued member of the family.

Hebrews 12:1-2

Therefore, since we are surrounded by so great a cloud of witnesses, let us also lay aside every weight, and sin which clings so closely, and let us run with endurance the race that is set before us, looking to Jesus, the Founder and Perfecter of our faith, who for the joy that was set before him endured the cross, despising the shame, and is seated at the right hand of the throne of God.

Lay Aside Every Weight

What are the weights in a mom's life?

- the weight of public opinion,
- the weight of regret,
- the weight of self doubt,
- the weight of "am I doing it right?"
- the weight of "am I enough?"
- the weight of loneliness and isolation,
- the weight of fear,
- the weight of worry and anxiety.

All of these weights are distractions.

When we believe the doubts and fears, we give them the power to hold us captive and weigh us down. Our greatest freedom comes when we realize that we have the power to release those weights. After all, they were never the truth anyway.

We live in a world full of distractions. One of the major problems for parents today is we are raising kids in a noisy world full of both challenges and opportunities that seem to cry out for our attention in a million different ways. One source of distraction is the vast amount of information that's available to us at our finger tips, we will refer to this as external noise. Then there's the noise in our heads from our own doubts and insecurities, we will refer to this an internal noise. The truth is, the external noise isn't nearly as loud as the noise in our heads.

When we are distracted and unfocused, our challenges can cause us to immediately seek advice from others on what they think we should do. An intentional parent takes the time to add a step to the process.

By all means, we should seek wisdom and advice from others. However, we should only ask for that input after we have taken the time to get crystal clear on what matters most to our family first. Then, any advice we seek should help us move forward to achieve that goal and purpose.

Without this crucial step, we run the risk of becoming incredibly overwhelmed. All the ideas and long how-to lists will rob us of the joy of being a parent. When we feel overwhelmed with all we feel we "have to do" to be a "good mom," we have probably picked up a lot of good advice, but perhaps not necessarily the best advice for our family.

Our families are unique; therefore, the way we parent and lead our families will also be unique. In fact, not only are our families unique but the children within our families are unique too. If we have more than one child, we already know, what worked for one child doesn't always work the same way for the next, even though they are being raised in the same household.

Perhaps this is God's way of ensuring that we have to prayerfully seek Him every step of the way. If there were a parenting manual that guaranteed we could achieve pre-scripted results, we would no longer need Him. Instead we must spend time in God's Word and in prayer seeking Him for what we should do next.

We must deeply committed to our core values and living a life of purpose, while holding loosely the reins of the process. May we take the time to define what's most important concerning our family, take the time to talk through and develop our intention, and then prayerfully seek out the tools and advice to help us achieve that.

Be deeply committed to your core values, but hold loosely the reins of the process.

In our home:

One day I realized that no matter how much I loved my kids, God our Father loved them even more than I ever could. That a-ha moment set me free. Sometimes I still make the mistake of believing that the weight of their future as an adult is on my shoulders. I feel like if I don't make the right choices for them, their lives will be ruined, and it'll all be my fault. I tend to overly concern myself with the food they eat, the friends they hang out with, the TV shows they watch, the books they read, etc. causing   myself more and more stress worry, and anxiety. All of these symptoms are a clue that I'm distracted and not living according to God's plan. He promised to leave His children love, joy, peace, patience, kindness, and more. None of those are present when I think that successfully parenting my kids is all up to me. I must teach them to depend on God. My life's purpose is to remind them that God has a purpose and a plan for their lives and He will reveal it in due time.

Releasing the Weights that Hold us Down

Great families are not great because the parents are extraordinary people, but because the parents consistently do extraordinary things. That's good news. This means creating a great family is possible for not just a special few, but for all of us.

We don't have to be amazingly patient, organized, or talented. Instead, we must choose day-by-day to do things that break the ordinary off our actions and redeem them to their rightful place of purpose. We must continually release those weights that hold us down and cause us to stumble.

That's being an intentional parent, one who creates an extraordinary family.

Every parent we have ever admired and looked up to has one thing in common. They each had a trait that stood out and captured our attention. Even if we couldn't put our finger on it, there was a certain something that made them remarkable, and the object of our envy. The greatest trait they each possessed was they were intentional.

They found purpose and meaning for their family. Maybe it was in sports or music, or volunteering or business. Or perhaps in spite of busy schedules they organized the family schedule to ensure they ate dinner together every night. Another family may have a regular family Bible study. Either way, they caught our eye. We witnessed an intentional parent.

Creating a great family is possible, not just for a special few, but for all of us.

In our home:

People often ask us how we were able to build a successful business that retired my husband from his corporate job. After all, we built this business while living on one income and having 7 children along the way. What we often share is that business is a part of our family. It's as natural a part of our conversation as I would imagine politics is for the Bush family or sports for Michael Jordan's family. Whenever our family is in the car or around the dinner table, we love to discuss business and real estate. Business is our family interest. It's part of who we are. We think up business ideas and strategies the way others who are gifted in cooking might come up with new recipes. When people hear our story I often tell them, the real estate business is not for everyone. What they admire is not really about our family, it's the intentional living that's at-tractive. Their work is discovering where they too can be more inten-tional within their own family.

The Ever Elusive Search To Be a 'Good Mom'

I remember when my son was a baby. I felt a lot of fear of Sudden Infant Death Syndrome, also known as SIDS. It was a condition where babies would die in their sleep and no one had a real explanation for why. All new parents were advised that babies should sleep on their side.

There was a doctor-approved, triangular foam filled pillow, designed to prop babies up on their side when sleeping. A few years later the advice on how to prevent SIDS had changed. The new advice was to have babies sleep on their back and not on their sides. No more pillow wedge device. In fact, no items in the bed at all, except the baby and perhaps a light blanket.

I remember the panic I felt thinking I had endangered my older kids because they slept on their sides, while also fearing that this new advice might also be wrong. Either way, I felt trapped, because deep down I wanted to do the 'right thing'. If it wasn't sleep positions that plagued me, then it was the 'right' car seat, the 'right' food, the 'right' schools, or any number of decisions.

After all, I wanted to be a "good mom."

We all know the :good mom":
- Is always patient
- Never yells or gets angry
- Always prepares hot, nutritious meals
- Never allows her children to eat junk food
- Is always confident
- Is a great hostess
- Is a fabulous home decorator
- Can hold a conversation on politics, business, finance, and current events
- Is completely aware of her child's development ages and stages
- Always smiles
- Is prepared with the appropriate consequence for misbehavior
- Chooses the best school for her children
- Only reads the choicest literature to her family
- Lives in a great neighborhood
- Has a thriving marriage
- Volunteers in several non-profits
- Has intense daily Bible study
- Never runs out of milk, cheese, bread, or other pantry staples

- Never offends
- Never misunderstands
- Never forgets
- Never shames
- Exercises daily
- Is not overweight
- Has incredible friendships that last for years
- Always places her children's needs before her own
- Spends lots of time with her child
- And on, and on, and on!

If given the time and the space, there could be so much more added to this list. It is by no means an exhaustive list, but it is *exhausting*.

The list not only could go on for pages and pages--it also changes. When our children are little, we have one definition of a good mom, and as our children get older the list changes. It's tough enough being a mom without having to carry around the added mental baggage of constantly feeling like we fall short.

In the ever elusive search to be a "good mom", we believe that there's something we need to do in order to be good enough. Our response is to try our best to make things great on the outside, when our greatest battlefield is fought in our hearts and minds.

When we take the time to get clear on what really matters, our core values and our intentions will lead the way and set the agenda. Our best actions will always be a result of a clear intention first, then we can seek to discover the tools that will help us reach our intended goal.

When we miss that key piece, we run the risk of taking lots of action and getting lots of stuff done, only to realize we didn't create results we really want for our family.

Like the mom who has her kids in multiple activities and they rarely eat at home. She feels guilty for feeding her kids tons of fast food, but she can't figure out how to do things differently. Or the mom with the thriving career, yet her growing success means that she sees her kids less and less. Or the mom with the well decorated house that is admired by all of her friends because it's always spotless. However, deep down no one knows she feels unappreciated and taken for granted.

When we take the time to determine what really matters before moving forward, we will love the results we get every single time.

The mom who wants a clean house may also want her family to express how thankful they are to her and show their appreciation for a clean home by helping to keep the home clean. Imagine how much happier and free this mom would feel to have her family helping out around the house. That can happen.

When we get clear and focused on being an intentional parent, we will no longer settle for partial results like, the house is clean, but I had to do it all myself. Instead we can get full results like a clean home, with everyone chipping in.

> *It's tough enough being a mom without having to carry around the added mental baggage of constantly feeling like you fall short.*

In our home:

I have 7 children, and each one of them has a list of
chores and responsibilities. At the time of this writing, I
cook breakfast every day, and dinner only 2 days a week.
This is after years of teaching my children how to help
out around the house. I never wanted to create a home
where I was the kids' maid and their job was simply to
hang out while I busily worked around them as they
lounged. Instead, I taught them from a pretty young age
that they helped to create the mess in the home and they
were expected to help clean it up. Even a toddler can pick
up a few toys or put their napkin in the trash. I was
constantly on the lookout for little jobs that I could pass
on to the kids. My experience is that productive kids feel
valued and appreciated. And without responsibilities,
children tend to feel tolerated, and they question their
value and ability to handle real work.

The Weight of Deception

I'm the only one with this struggle
I'm not cut out for this
I should probably have this all figured out by now
It would be so much easier if only...
My mistakes define me as a parent
Other parents are doing a much better job than me

A lie is not always obvious. No matter how subtle the lie, it not only affects us, but our entire family. Those lies impact our decisions, our view of the future, and our memory of the past.

Here's the truth about lies :
- They are not true Psalms 25:5
- They are only true to those who believe them Acts 14:2
- Lies can only deceive those who believe them James 1:16
- Our enemy, the deceiver, is behind every single one John 8:44
- Lies have one goal: to get us to miss our purpose John 10:10

Take a look at the six lies parents believe and think about how believing those lies affects every decision, how they view their family's future and past, and the amount of hope they feel regarding their kids.

1. I'm the only one with this struggle

You are never the only one. The same challenges you face today, other parents around the world have them too. Perhaps some of the parents who are close to you, like your friends currently share that issue. It could be they're just not willing to admit it. You are not alone.

2. I'm not cut out for this.

You are stronger than you think and more capable than you give yourself credit for. You may not feel like the "right person for the job," and that's real. But the truth is, out of all the moms in the world, you were chosen for this unique assignment. And that means there's something in you that is an exact match for the challenges you are facing. Have a good cry if you need to. Then wipe your tears and rise to the challenge. Use every fiber of your talents, skills, and resources to meet the challenges head on. You were chosen for this, and that was no mistake.

3. I should probably have this all figured out by now.

As our kids get older, we sometime feel like we should
have a few things figured out by now. Only as they get
older, we find the exact opposite to be true. Here's the
truth- there's no such thing as having it "all figured out."
Parenting is personal development training at its finest.
There's no end to the process of transformation and
learning. We don't arrive. We choose to embrace the
journey. Learn today's lesson and eagerly anticipate a
new one tomorrow. It's a process of discovery.

4. It would be so much easier if.....

If I had more money. If I had more time. If I had girls. If I
had boys. If my kids were older. If my kids were younger.
If I was younger, smarter, richer, had more energy. It
would be so much easier.

Few people would put the words parenting and easy in
the same sentence. No matter what circumstances we
face, parenting is hard work, pure and simple. Some face
more challenges than others, but it is hard work for all of
us. What makes the difference is when we focus on parenting on purpose. Parenting is not easier if all of our
preferences are met. Parenting gets easier the moment
we choose to parent our children on purpose, in spite of
the circumstances and challenges we face.

5. I've made too many mistakes

Mistakes are a sign that we're trying. Mistakes give us feedback on the decisions we've made. Our mistakes don't define us. They are not an indicator of our capability as a parent. Not at all. They are mere messengers sent to give us a response to a past decision. We have the power to assign meaning to our recent feedback.

Burning dinner doesn't have to mean we can't cook. And forgetting to pay a bill doesn't have to mean we suck at handling money. We are the ones assigning those meanings. Since we are choosing the meaning, let's be sure to choose a kind one. Burnt dinner can simply mean we won't eat what we planned for dinner that night. And forgetting to pay a bill can mean we need to set up a reminder system for paying our bills.

We will continually make mistakes, let us remind one another that our mistakes are not final, they're only feedback.

6. Other parents are doing a much better job than me.

Ahhh …comparison, the thief of joy. We may be doing an excellent job with our kids, but then we look to the left and to the right and suddenly our best doesn't seem all that great. When we're already struggling to do the best we can, even the hint that someone is doing things better can make us feel so defeated. That secret fear that maybe we're not doing the best for our children can get any of us to feel down and defeated.

When we are distracted and focused on what other parents are doing with their kids, we are less likely to stay know what is right for our own. We are more likely to deny our own purpose and the purpose for our family, eventually leaving that purpose unfulfilled in this world.

> *When we focus on what other parents are doing with their kids, we are less likely to know what is right for our own.*

The Weight Of Comparison

There are those who are drowning in the busyness, and distractions of life, and then there are those who rise above it. We tend to describe those who rise, as the successful parents. They become our go-to examples of the parents who are doing it 'right.' The ones who have it all together.

After all, their kids would never scream bloody murder in the grocery store. In fact, their babies slept through the night at three weeks old while the rest of us struggled to get our toddler to quit waking up. Their kids always have on matching shoes and socks, while our kids, well....don't- our kids have on shoes OR socks. Their kids get good grades in school and become captain of the school team, while our kids think farting is a sport.

But the truth is the parents we idolize and secretly doubt ever have any problems, have challenges too. Areas where the noise threatens to drown out their sense of purpose and connection to a clear vision for their family.

We can't tell if someone's rising simply by looking at how things look on the outside. Rising is something that happens deep within. It happens when we tap into our strengths, our gifts, and our talents. When we live in alignment with the core values that move us, motivate us and mean the most to us – we intentionally shed the weight of comparison and rise. The weight of comparison no longer holds us down.

In order to rise, we must first release what holds us down.

The challenges we face as parents, are not necessarily a sign that we're doing anything wrong or that God is mad at us, but instead each challenge becomes the exact fuel we need to rise to our greatest potential, while living true to our God-given purpose.

God promised that He would never give us more than we can handle. Therefore, any challenge He has sent our way, He has already given us the grace to handle. We have everything we need to successfully face any challenge. Nothing is missing. We are not broken or deficient.

Let's not believe the lies of the enemy that we must compare ourselves to one another. We were each hand picked. Maybe we just need to discover more of the gifts and talents placed within us when we were in our mother's womb. Together, let's resist the urge to shrink back. This is our time to rise.

The challenges we face as parents are real. In no way do I want to glaze over how daunting this task can be. And that's exactly why I challenge each of us to rise. It's going to require us to be on purpose and to be intentional. We are going to have to let go of the weights that hold us down and shut out the noise that seeks to distract us.

In our home:

In the past, our family seemed like the ones who "had it all together." Our kids were seen being well behaved, polite, and respectful. They got good grades. They excelled at their interests. What a joy, right?! Nope. You see, for the longest time I struggled with anger. Many times my kids were well behaved because they didn't want their mommy to lose her temper and get upset. I have seen the look of horror in my kids eyes as I fussed at them for making a mistake. I have had my kids avoid me, and for good rea-son.

Thankfully being an angry mom is no longer my is-sue, but the fact is, I still have issues. That's a fact of life. If those moms knew that what they envied was the result of an angry mom, they would probably not envy this quite so much. That's why looking at the outside is not a good measurement of whether a family is rising or drowning.

The Weight of Distraction

There's so much stuff to do. We run the risk of getting stuff done while missing out on the most important work of creating a powerful family.

Busyness is a distraction.

Being busy and living a life of purpose are not the same thing. On the outside they may look very similar. But below the surface things are radically different. Busy is a continual act of going and doing with no pause or reflection on our purpose.

Living a life of purpose is a continual search for meaning. Knowing our "why" lays the foundation for each decision we make. We may find that as we sort through the busy-ness in our lives that not too many things change. However, the reason we do things changes, and that is what's important.

Whether things on the outside change a lot or a little is not the point. The real issue is whether our families are living with a sense of purpose or just being busy? We must be honest.

There is a direct correlation between our commitment to being intentional by living a life of purpose, and our family's ability to break free from distractions. The more we connect each part of our lives to our core values and our purpose, the less we are weighed down with distraction.

The more we connect each part of our lives to our core values, and our purpose - the less we are weighed down with distraction.

The Weight of Public Opinion

Many moms reach out to me as a mentor looking for ways to be intentional with their family. They want help. They want things to be better.

When I ask them to describe what they think is wrong, I get a multitude of answers, from toddler issues, to teen problems.

The most common challenge to them solving the problem is the weight of needing others' approval. Many moms share with me ideas on how they could ease their busy schedules, but immediately they wonder – "What will *they* think?" They question whether their friends, neighbors, and family will approve. It's amazing to see how quickly they shut down at the thought of losing the approval of others.

As moms, we must release the need for others to approve of us. It's always easy for us to think that something is wrong when we're listening to another person's definition of what it means to be right.

Instead, our life's work is to simply embrace God's standard as our sole definition for our family. The short leash of public opinion will always keep the freedom our family desires just beyond our reach. And the biggest crime is that opinions change quickly and often. It's a game we can never win.

When we embrace God's standard, we embrace the grace, freedom, creativity, and fun that comes with it. There's no burden when we walk in God's ways. He created each one of us with unique gifts and strengths. He gave each one of us goals, ambitions, and passions. When we simply accept that we are unique in the way that we've been created, there's no need to carry the burden of hoping that others will approve. Our fear-based seeking of approval and acceptance from others only leaves us feeling empty and lost. But when we release the need to fit in by embracing our unique calling, we can easily see that God's approval is all we ever need.

The Weight of Too Much Information

As we sense God making our purpose clear, we must be willing to make bold, daring moves. A life of action is a life of faith. Have faith that God called us to be an intentional parent, and that He is faithful to be with us every step of the way.

After we go to seminars or read a few books, we get all excited about the ideas we learned, but often we fail to ask one important question: Is this right for me? Is this right for my family?

This book is no exception. While reading, be sure to ask the question: Is this right for my family?

Let's not make the mistake of equating a good idea with God's plan. A whole lot of good ideas will cease to be good the moment we try to walk out our purpose while carrying around the extra weight of too many good ideas. Too much information is a distraction that will cause us to miss out on God's best plan. Let's allow good ideas to inspire us and broaden our sense of possibility, as we prayerfully seek God's plan for our family.

An idea is only good when it is God-inspired. Anything short of God's will and plan will sorely disappoint. When we're following the path He has chosen for us, we receive His greatest blessings.

Every day we will be tempted to look to others with the hope to simply rinse and repeat what worked for them. Even good results from this approach will pale in comparison to what was possible if we took the time to ask: "Is this for me? Is this for my family?"

The Weight of Perfection

Deep down, we all want to avoid making mistakes. For some reason, we believe that in order to be a good mom, we fear letting our children down and becoming the reason they ultimately don't succeed in life.

We desperately want to avoid wrecking our children's lives, so we decide that if we parent correctly and do it the "right way," then our their lives will be good. We equate a good life as a life that's free from all hurt, harm, danger, and disappointment. But what if the things we see as "bad" for our kids are some of the best things they could ever experience?

What if those struggles, challenges, frustrations, and disappointments are exactly what they need to experience in order to become amazing adults?

Likewise, what if our parenting mistakes are exactly what our children need to see to truly understand that mistakes are not final-- they're only feedback? Perhaps our mistakes are the perfect example of the truth that messing up does not have the final say on our future. Our past is not the sole predictor of our potential. Our mess-ups are only a small part of the journey, and every part of the journey can be used for good.

If we think that it's all up to us to raise our kids, we will carry the heavy burden of perfection, believing that we must do everything right. There was only one perfect One. His name is Jesus.

So there's hope for those of us who have made plenty of mistakes. Be encouraged. Let's allow our mistakes to become lessons. Let's choose to see them as opportunities to learn and grow. We can take each mistake and leverage it for good.

Mistakes without hope leave us feeling stuck. They bury us under the ugliness of despair and the weight of perfection, choking out our true potential. But when we see our mistakes as part of the journey, we become free. Our past mess-ups no longer hold us captive. The message of hope sets us free. Rejoice in the opportunity to grow and mature.

We can capture our negative thoughts and replace them with the truth. We are all growing and learning, and that means sometimes we will mess up. But that's okay, because parenting is not a journey of perfection.

In our home:

I often refer to parenting as the Refiner's Fire. This is
based on a poem I read years ago. In the poem it
described the process of a silversmith who was heating
the silver in order to purify it for use. The more he
heated the silver, the more dross or impurities rose to the
surface, which he would then skim off and dispose.
Eventually an observer asked the silversmith when he
knew the process was complete, and his response was,
when I can see my image in the pan. I believe that God is
using my family to turn up the heat. Over the years I
have had all kinds of impurities rise to the surface--
selfishness, greed, envy, jealousy, anger, you name it.
Some of the hardest times of my life have felt exactly like
someone was turning up the heat and I rarely liked what
came out of me in those moments. The Refiner's Fire is
real for me, and it's exactly what I needed. It's the process
I needed but would never voluntarily sign up for.
Because of my family, I have become more patient, kind,
accepting, and forgiving. This journey has not been one
of perfection, but I have come to realize that the journey
itself is all a part of God's plan and process in order to see
His likeness in me.

SECTION 3

Run The Race With Endurance

Ask Better Questions

By asking better questions, we can find the advice that best suits our family-- quicker, sooner, faster. We can skip the trial and error methods that currently take up a lot of our time and energy. And we can be more consistent in how we parent our children because we've taken the time to determine what's most important for our family's needs.

We desire to live each day with a greater sense of purpose and that means we must find ways that our family can live true to our own unique set of core values.

It's a discovery process. It's a journey. We don't get the full details up front; we must walk it out day-by-day. This could be the single most frustrating thing in this book so far. But it's true. We won't ever have the full details up front. It's a process that requires our trust and diligence.

However, what we do have is the ability to make a decision. When we are unsure of what question to ask or the next step to take, just make a decision. Whether it's right or wrong, we will find out soon enough. As we investigate the feedback our decisions are giving us we can evaluate if we like the results. If we don't like the results, we get to make a new decision. And keep making a new decision until we feel like we're getting results that are in line with our God-given purpose.

If we're following parenting advice and we don't like the results it's producing, we must adapt it to fit our family or seek out a whole new direction. We must always stay true to what's most important for our family.

If we're following parenting advice and we don't like the results it's producing, we must adapt it to fit our family or seek out a whole new direction.

Understand Responsibility

There's a huge difference between taking personal responsibility and taking the blame. When we are distracted and feeling overwhelmed, we are more likely to confuse the two.

While we are responsible for our own actions, thoughts, and emotions, we are not responsible for other people's thoughts, actions, and emotions. When we forget this truth, we live our lives trying to control others, and we create unhealthy relationships within the family.

When we are intentional, we are more likely to take personal responsibility for the part we played.

The more we live on the intentional end of the continuum, the more we can keep our minds and hearts clear enough to give the best response. Brooke Castillo, Master Life Coach and Trainer, once broke the word responsibility down like this - "Response-ability." Our ability to respond is at it's greatest when we are being intentional and less distracted. At the foundation, personal responsibility comes from a place of ownership and acceptance. It always serves to move us forward.

If we ever find ourselves unsure of whether we are blaming instead of taking personal responsibility, check-in. Is the focus on our own actions or on someone or something else? Other people cannot make us happy. And they cannot make us mad, without our permission. They cannot make us feel loved. And they cannot make us feel rejected without our consent.

We can influence one another. Our children influence us all the time. It's easy to think their whining causes us to yell, or their constant questions make us feel annoyed. In reality, their actions and emotions do not cause us to yell or feel annoyed, unless we give them permission. As the parent, we get the opportunity to help our children manage their actions and emotions, while we are in the process of managing our own. That's what can make being a parent so humbling. We sense how much work we still need to do to better manage our own lives, while we have little people looking for us to provide guidance to them at the same time.

Response-ability:

The ability to keep our hearts and mind clear enough to give the best response.

Set the Standard

Parenting is a huge commitment. As parents, we set the bar in our homes. Our lives set the standard. How we live and the choices we make define for our kids what's possible in life and what life is all about.

Our kids catch on fast. As they watch us live our lives, they determine the family standard not by what we say, but by how we live.

Intentional parents understand this to be true, and allow this truth to motivate them to constantly seek to better their best. It all begins with us--the parents. We cannot expect character traits in our kids that we, their parents, are not willing to also pursue in our own lives.

- We cannot expect our children to be kind, if we are not.
- We cannot expect our children to be creative, if we are not.
- We cannot expect our children to be generous, if we are not.

It all starts with us, the parents.

As parents, we set the context for our family. We get to help our children see that although we are not 100% perfect in our pursuit, we can still strive for excellence. Our job is to provide a vision of what's possible. Then we encourage our kids to do their best to outpace our efforts. We allow them to stand on the shoulders of our wisdom and past experiences as they reach higher than we ever could. They'll go so much farther, so much faster--all because they had intentional, purposeful parents.

Though our intentional lives can set the stage for our children's success, there are no promises in this journey. We can model purpose and intention for our children all their lives, but in the end, they must choose. Our role is to influence our family to live a life of purpose. We work hard to make our standards and core values appealing. But in the end, they get to choose whether or not to follow our lead. This can be the most challenging and disheartening part of the journey. We can do our absolute best, yet our children might choose a different path. It's at this point that we get to say- "I did the best I could with what I knew to do."

Let's pour grace on our kids. If they choose not to follow our lead, encourage them to live their best life with what they know while always seeking to live a life of purpose.

Speak The Truth In Love

Our voices are so important in the lives of everyone in our family. If we see trouble on the horizon, it's not loving to remain to silent. Bad habits, wrong relationships, or laziness are signs of trouble on the horizon, and the most loving thing we can do is speak up.

As moms, quite often we can see trouble a mile away. We are the ones who get the opportunity to speak loving correction to our children. Our voices are a first line of defense for us. Our protection comes in the form of warning, watching for those who are drifting along and are no longer connected to the family, those who are not engaged and plugged in. We look for areas where love ties have been weakened or even broken by misunderstanding, sarcasm, teasing, and disagreements. We see those things and we get to use our voices to speak a message rooted in love.

Law enforcement officials, the military, and other organizations within our society work diligently to protect us. Their mission is protection, but their main motivation is not love. As moms, we step up to protect our families because we love our families. When we see them in harm's way, making choices that lead to pain, disappointment, hurt, and brokenness in their lives- we speak up. It's the most loving thing we could ever do. It is a demonstration of our hearts for our families when we speak up and share what we see happening in their lives.

All of us can be blinded to our own failings and weaknesses. Our hearts are easily deceived. We all tend to believe we are stronger than we are. We believe we're smarter than we are. We convince ourselves that we've got things all figured out. Our greatest deception is that we don't need others to help us, because we can do it all by ourselves. An independent, self-reliant life is the ultimate deception.

As moms we get to speak into the lives of our family with love and say, "The moment we think we have it all figured out, we don't." "We were not created to live an independent self-reliant life. The greatest gift God could ever give us is a family. And as your mom I love you enough to speak up and call out Danger! Danger! Not only when there's physical danger present, but also when it's on the horizon of your heart and mind."

Love is patient. Love is kind. We all love to encourage this part of the love message. But there's another part that is equally important. That's the honest part of the love message. If we are not honest and authentic, our children will not trust us. Our children can sense when we're trying to hide the truth behind a sweet smile and kind words. We consider that loving them, but they sense we are hiding something. Deep down they know things aren't right, they're just not sure exactly what's wrong. They know something's not right, but they're not clear what.

Let's be loving-- the gentle and kind way. And let's be loving-- the honest and true way too. That's the way to build real relationship with our children.

When it's time for us to have one of those hard conversations with our kids due to disobedience or them making poor choices, let's remind ourselves that hard conversations can be the most loving thing we can do for our kids. When they disobey or make poor choices in life, they don't need us to protect them from the truth. Instead we get to help them face the truth which will help them grow and mature. Let's not hide behind kindness and a smile due to our own limited understanding of love.

Let love be the motivator to move forward and have the conversation, not an excuse to avoid it. Avoidance is not a loving act. Keeping our children ignorant at times when they need information is not a loving act. It may protect us and make us feel better, but serving our own needs at the expense of what our children need in the moment, is not the loving thing to do. Love is gentle and kind AND love is honest and true. It is both. Have the hard conversation, do it. It's the loving thing to do.

Love can handle the sweet conversations and love can handle the hard ones too. There doesn't have to be an either or choice. If we want to have a good relationship with our children, we must honest and real conversation with them. They will trust us all the more.

If they don't sense we are willing to be honest with them, they are not going to be real with us. Broken relationships are rooted in a lack of trust. Speaking the truth in love protects our families, builds trusting relationships, and sets our families up to be intentional in every way.

Rephrase the Problem

Every problem and challenge within our family is linked to an underlying question that begs to be answered. The question is just beneath the surface. And it's the same for every challenge. How can I be an intentional parent in this moment?

When we are intentional, we easily recognize moments that are ripe opportunities for growth and maturity not only in our children, but ourselves as well. Even when our children's needs may be inconvenient or their behavior may be embarrassing, they need us to be the parent. Unfortunately these teachable moments don't usually come at a convenient time that easily fits our schedule. But that doesn't change that our children are depending on us to show them the right way.

The next time we find ourselves in the midst of a parenting challenge, or shall we call it a training opportunity, let's be willing to pause long enough to ask, "how can I be an intentional parent in this moment?" or" how can I bring purpose and meaning to this moment?"

Seeking Expert Advice

When life gets really busy, our desperation for relief can cause us to seek advice from a place of unworthiness. We begin to see ourselves as incapable and we seek advice by saying things like "I have no idea what to do. Someone please, just tell me what to do." But God didn't call someone else to raise our kids. He called us. He didn't make a mistake. We are more capable than we give ourselves credit for.

Can we benefit from the knowledge and wisdom of others? Yes. However, there's a difference between seeking advice by saying something like "Tell me what to do, because I have no clue. I'm lost and I'm don't think I can do this!" when we could say " I trust that you have something to say that will help me. I'm ready to listen and take notes."

The first parent will listen, go home, and try to do everything the person they believe to be an expert, told them to do. When things don't work out as they hoped, any disappointment simply reinforces their initial doubts about their ability as a parent. "See, I told you I couldn't do this!" Or " I knew this wouldn't work."

The Intentional Parent's approach sounds more like this: "I believe you have something to say that can help me."

Intentional parents are willing to sift through the information shared with them and look for the golden nuggets, those juicy pieces of advice that provide a solution that matches the family's core values. They are willing to prayerfully test each piece of advice. If one idea doesn't work, they don't assume that the failure was due to being incapable or deficient in any way. They simply say, "this idea is not for our family. It's not a fit." They don't allow the fact that a particular idea wasn't a fit for their family to mean anything about their parenting skills.

Building a Team Work Attitude

Make a list of all the things that need to get done today. Overwhelming isn't it? There are more things on the to-do list than could ever possibly get done in one 24 hour day. It's called a time constraint. We only have 24 hours in a day, yet our schedules and plans don't reflect that. Over and over again we create impossible schedules and then feel frustrated at the end of the day when we see how many things never get done.

Many times we resist limits. Limits tell us that we can't do it all, and honestly that's a frustrating message. So we seek out time management tips and tools to distract us from the truth that 'doing it all' is simply not possible.

What do we do when we finally accept that we can't get it all done?

First we celebrate. The simple fact that we are willing to admit we can't get it all done is a huge moment in time that few people ever experience. Most people are deter-mined to prove they can handle it. If they work harder, longer, and faster they can overcome time limits. However, if we want something new, we have to do things in a new way.

There's one phrase that is not allowed in the Seay household and it's this- "That's not my job!" As soon as someone says this, they're job list doubles. This statement reflects a 'me' mentality, when the goal is to create a 'we' mentality of teamwork. When we work together as a team, everyone wins. Teamwork causes us to not only look out for ourselves, but to look out for the needs of others too.

After celebration the next move is to enroll the family. It's time to start delegating tasks for each person to complete as part of the team. Moms, let's not try to manage the home all by ourselves. It's too much to ask of ourselves, and it's asking too little of our families.

There's an African proverb that reads, "if you want to go fast go alone, if you want to go far, go with others." It seems counter-intuitive to our independent, self-made mindsets that working with others is a better plan. We want to believe that we can do it ourselves. But we were not designed to do things on our own. We need each other.

I need you. You need me.

Read that statement again.

Now say it out loud.

Family life is preparing our children to live the rest of their lives with intention. Let's prepare them to resist any distractions that pull them away from a focus on purpose, helping them to understand that it's impossible for any of us to live purposeful lives in isolation. Apart from connection to others, purpose and meaning die a slow death. To the extent that we are involved in the lives of others we thrive and become an encouragement to others.

Every day we have the opportunity to use our time and talents for the benefit of those around us, especially our families.

It's impossible for us to live purposeful lives in isolation.

The Standard of Capable

I can't!
I can't do it!
I t-r-i-e-d!
Moooommmm! Help me!

We've all been there--those times when our children
our children are learning a new skill like how to tie their
shoes, ride a bike, or hold a fork properly. The
frustration they feel leads to whiny voices and quick
tempers. If we're not careful, their emotions can begin to
rub off on us. We begin to get whiny and angry too.

We usually will make one of two choices:

1. we will give in to make the whining stop, or
2. we will raise our voices, and yell louder than
   them, just to be heard.

But what is happening beneath the surface?

There is a struggle taking place within the heart of the
child and the parent.

79

The child is asking:
- Can I do it?
- Is this too much?
- Can't someone just do it for me instead?

The parent is wondering:
- Can they *really* do it, or am I pushing them too hard?
- Is this too much?
- Should I just help them this time?

This is a great time to introduce a tool called the standard of capable.

The standard of capable is simply the belief that another person is capable of more than they believe in this moment. They do not need to be rescued. In fact, offering to help too quickly robs them of the chance to reach their full potential. Give them the space to figure things out, while keeping a watchful eye for signs of exhaustion or unhealthy self-talk.

This standard assumes that instruction has been given and the needed resources have been provided. Once this happens, we must resist the urge to rescue and instead lean on the standard of capable.

Instead ask the following:

- Have I provided them enough instruction?
- Have I provided them with the tools they need?
- Have I communicated that they are capable and I believe in them?

If we can answer yes to these questions, it's time to step back. The struggle we are about to witness is necessary because it gives birth to confidence, resourcefulness, creativity, and self-worth. To the untrained eye it looks like frustration, anger, and an overall hot mess. But look closer. Keep a watchful eye. There's something happening beneath the surface, and we'll miss it if we move in too soon.

The standard of capable allows us to accept that challenge and struggle are part of the journey. Avoiding that struggle only serves to weaken a person. Anyone who is regularly rescued becomes a person who:

- easily quits
- seeks the easy way out
- makes excuses
- doesn't try very hard
- avoids challenges and things that are new
- manipulates with tears, whining, and constant cries for help

Be committed enough to their growth to not step in and break the process by rescuing them. Instead, keep a watchful, loving eye on their struggle. This is exactly what they need to grow and mature.

Our Voice: The Power to Influence

So many moms are great care-takers, loving supporters, and great assistants, but struggle to use their voice. They find it hard to speak up and express themselves. It's not because they don't have great things to say, but because they fear saying it wrong or hurting someone's feelings.

It's important that the mother's voice is both heard and listened to. She has the pulse of the family. She is the one who knows what's really happening in the home. She can tell you her kids' faults and strengths.

In the pursuit of intentional parenting, finding her voice is part of the journey. She is not merely giving good suggestions to the family, but casting a vision. Moms must commit to speak up and use their voices.

Here are a few ideas for moms who struggle with being heard:

1. **Remember your words matter.** Your words are infused with wisdom from God. They are not merely good ideas. Your words have the power to protect, encourage, strengthen, and guide. Strong words deserve a strong voice.

2. **Having a strong and powerful voice is not the same as shouting.** Often shouting and yelling are a cover up for a person's insecurities. To be powerful there's no need to yell and scream. Instead, speak with authority and clarity.

3. **Respect your words and require others to do the same.** Teach your children to honor your position by listening to what you have to say. Don't allow them to speak over you or turn their backs when you're talking. It's not okay for them to mock you or ignore your words. You must teach them to respectfully listen to what you have to say.

4. **Resist the urge to go on and on.** Don't let a thought or idea get too long. It's easy to go from extreme of under sharing, to other ditch of

over-sharing. Be concise when sharing thoughts and opinions. Stay on topic.

5. **Your ability to effectively share our thoughts is directly related to your ability to get your family's attention.** Without attention, there's no communication. There are many ways to get your family's attention. Be creative, but guard against creativity undermining the seriousness of the message. If you have something serious to share, get their attention in a way that communicates a serious tone. If you have something fun to share, get their attention in a fun way. Let the message drive the strategy for getting their attention.

6. **Check in to make sure they understand.** After speaking, ask them what they heard. This will minimize miscommunication and ensure they don't just bob their heads up and down at the sound of your voice. Confirm that they are present and engaged with what you are sharing.

Ever heard the saying, "you teach people how to treat you?" It's true. And this includes your children.

You are teaching your children how to treat you. You teach them what's okay and what's not okay. If you feel like your kids don't listen to you or obey you, the truth is, you have allowed that behavior. You have taught them to believe that is acceptable.

On some level you have undermined your own authority and leadership, and given them permission to make their own decisions. Unfortunately a child-led decision is based on their limited view, limited life experience, and limited maturity-- all of which lead to poor decision making skills.

It's time to reclaim your voice. If your kids aren't listening to you, stop being so easy to ignore. If your kids don't do what you say, don't allow them the opportunity to do anything else until they do as you asked. If your kids are taking you for granted and treating you like a maid and a servant, you have the power to change that.

You are teaching them to treat you that way. You have allowed this behavior and it has created the results you see today. If you don't like the results, it's time to change things up.

Ever driven by a business with a sign that says, "Under New Management"? That sign lets the community know that the business is the same, but the way they do things has changed. I love to tell moms to take the same approach. Let your family know that things are a-changin' around here.

The 4 Emotions that precede all poor communication

Think back to a recent misunderstanding, conflict, or a frustrating conversation. It's likely that one of four emotions were present. These four emotions affected either the words that were said or the way the message was heard. Perhaps both. Being aware of these four emotions can us help avoid many frustrating situations in the future.

We've all over-reacted few times. Like when the kid's chores are not done and the house is a mess, and we lose it. There's a normal reaction to the house being a mess, and then there's an OVER reaction. Overreacting looks like a lecture that turns into punishment and privileges being removed, all because there was laundry that hadn't been done or the kitchen was a mess.

We're not talking about the times when we hold our children accountable. No, we're referring to those moments when we behave unreasonably. The times we know deep down in our heart we have taken things way too far, and it was really not that serious.

For example we can be yelling at our kids, but if the phone rings, we answer it with a pleasant, sweet voice. Or we could be fussing across the house, yet answer the front door and be friendly and smile. Those embarrassing moments when we are completely out of character and out of control, those are the moments when need to H.A.L.T.

The acronym H.A.L.T. has been taught in recovery programs for decades. It's a tool to help point out where we are vulnerable so that we can take steps to avoid destructive behavior. The acronym H.A.L.T. stands for Hungry, Angry, Lonely, and Tired. When we are feeling any one of these emotions, this is not the time to make major decisions or to confront our children. Instead, the first thing we must do is take care of our own needs.

If we're hungry, eat.
If we're angry, resolve our anger.
If we're lonely, remind ourselves that we're loved.
And if we're tired, get some rest.

Once we've met our needs, then we can tackle the issue of the laundry in the living room or the dirty kitchen. If the laundry is left undone and we're feeling tired when we notice it, the laundry will still be undone after we get some rest. If we're feeling hungry and we notice the kitchen is a mess, grab something quick to eat, then deal with the fact that the kitchen is a mess. It'll be there. If we're angry, deal with our anger and then we can talk to our kids. If we're feeling lonely, like no one cares, and we feel taken for granted, remind ourselves of just how much we are loved by an all-loving God. Get reconnected to other people. Reach out to a friend. Call and check in with somebody. It's important to fill our love tank first, then deal with the situation.

When these four emotions are present and we try to deal with things right away, we won't get the results we truly want. In fact, the situation may become all the more frustrating.

Be alert to the presence of these four emotions. See them as hints of disaster on the horizon. We can save ourselves unnecessary frustration, by taking the time to H.A.L.T., calm down, and honor our needs.

This simple 3-step plan sets us up to be awesome, purpose-driven, and intentional parents.

Core Values For The Family

Understanding Core Values

Core values are the fabric of who we are, the DNA of our family. They represent our innermost desires, dreams, and hopes. Behind everything we do and every activity we choose to be a part of, our core values are the driving factor.

Character is how we do things, while values are why we do things. Character is an expression. Core values are the motivation. Character is seen. Core values are felt. Character is applied. Core values are lived.

Character is the next ring outside the bulls-eye. It's close to core values, but not dead center. If we focus on character, we will get good results. However, when we take the time to nail down our core values, and make them an essential part of our family, we will reap results beyond measure.

Character training focuses on how to act, think, and behave, with no connection to heart. It's the difference between behavior modification techniques and getting to the heart of the matter. We want change to happen on the heart level. It's easy to teach someone how to say the right things. But it's a different ball game when you want them to say and do the right thing because on their own.

We don't want our kids to just look good on the outside, we want their hearts to be conditioned to choose good even when they're tempted to choose differently. In order to achieve this, we must focus on core values first, then work on how to live them out.

Core values are a tool every family needs to shift the family's direction from free flowing and unfocused to purpose-driven and intentional. When you take the time to choose core values within your family, you are setting up a filter for everything in your home.

They are a simple tool to help eliminate long lists of rules by condensing rules into a short list of three simple words that act as guidelines. The reason I suggest three is that the number three is doable. Too many words and you will forget them. Too few and it's hard to really set a clear vision for the family. Three is the ideal number of words to recall on a moment's notice.

To narrow down your entire family vision into three words, it will require you to focus. This task will require you to be clear on what's most important to your family.

A few helpful questions narrow down the list:

- What 3 values will you most want your kids to live out when they grow up?
- What 3 values do you want for them to have as adults?
- What 3 values act as a bulls-eye for the direction you want your family to go?
- What 3 values stand out as the most important in life?
- If you had to choose only 3 lessons to teach your children, what would they be?

Think about the last time you got mad. When your core values are violated you tend to react strongly. Core values are a deep part of who you are as a person. They are fundamental to how you see the world and how we operate in it. When another person violates a value that you hold dear, you will react strongly to protect it. Even when you haven't completed a formal process to identify what those core values are, they're in there. And they're controlling you whether you know it or not. It's time to unearth them and use them in an intentional way.

> *Core values are a deep part of you. They shape how you see the world and how you operate in it.*

Casting the Vision With Family Values

Choosing our family's core values is an act of leadership. We are symbolically raising a flag to serve notice to ourselves and the world, this is what we stand for. These core values will shape our family for generations to come.

As our children grow older, and prepare to step out into the world as an adult, the family values they grew up with will give them a practical tool to lead and guide their own family.

Choosing our core values is an act of casting vision. Vision is simply a mental picture of how we imagine the future. Our family vision is a mental picture that serves to unite our family with a common goal. This vision helps us to know we are headed in the right direction when life gets really busy. The vision created from our core values will unify the family at all times - both the good times, and the times that are more challenging and become a part of the legacy we leave our children.

Family core values also become a tool that helps our children to navigate the often tricky road of growing up. As they refer to the family's core values, they will have an invaluable tool to help them make the right choices.

Family values create an identity for our family. The Smith family is known for being honest, hard-working, and loyal. Or the Williams family is known for being humble, charitable, and hospitable. Our families will be known for something. Instead of developing a reputation by chance, we get to make a choice.

As we raise the bar for our family, watch as each member of the family rises to the challenge. This family culture that we are building doesn't just affect our homes, but our friends, neighbors, and our community. As more families commit to being intentional and living with purpose, we all benefit. The more families who parent on purpose, the better our schools, our churches, and our nation will be for it. With family core values, we have the ability not only to raise the bar for this generation, but to create a family culture that benefits our family for generations to come.

Choosing the 'Right' Core Values

We might fall for a very real trap when it comes to choosing the core values for our family. We may be tempted to believe that there is a perfect set of core values, and therefore we may want to compare our list to others. There is a perfect set of core values for every family, however they may not be the exact same as another family. And that's okay.

We may look at the list of potential values and assume that one value is better than another, when in reality they are all equally good.

For example, we may want to choose humble over another word like tenacious, assuming that humility is a better, kinder way. But if the desire for our family is to be tenacious, then choose tenacious. Remember, we get to choose what these values look like in our own home.

The key is to not exclude any of the values on the basis of a desire to pick just the 'right' values.

102 • SUSAN SEAY

Choose the three values that best sum up what you desire for your family.

Comparison is a trap. Resist the urge to share your final choices of core values with others until you are confident that you have chosen the best core values for your family.

One set of values is not better than another. Even if two families choose the exact same words for their core values each family will express them completely differently.

Let's honor each other's families by resisting the temptation to compare ourselves to one another.

Pushing Through Procrastination

The common thief of procrastination wants to prevent us from choosing. Choose anyway.

Procrastination may show up and tell us to choose later. Choose now.

Fear of making the wrong choice may tell us we're doing it wrong. Choose anyway.

Disagreement with our spouse may tempt us to delay the process. Talk it out, but choose anyway.

Frustration with choosing may make us want to skip this step altogether. Choose anyway.

Comparison to other families may cause us to doubt that we chose the 'right' words. Choose anyway.

Doubt may cause us to question whether what we chose is possible. Choose anyway.

Anxiety may pressure us to choose the values that seem easy. Choose the challenging values that will stretch your family.

5 Areas to Use Our Core Values

As moms, there are five core areas we are managing at any given time. Across the board, for every mom, no matter how many kids, no matter the size of her home, or what stage of parenting, these 5 areas apply to every single one of us.

1. **Children:** The people that we care for each day. This may also include any loved ones like aging parents, for example. This includes anyone we are directly responsible for each day, not children who may have moved out on their own.

2. Our **homes:** The care and management of our homes, including everything that happens under our roof.—the routine upkeep, maintenance, repairs, remodeling, etc. This also includes having friends and family to visit, parties, celebrations, holidays, etc. Anything that happens underneath our roof to make our home a place that our family enjoys is part of this area.

3. **Family activities**: anything that happens away from home. If we must leave our home to be a part of these activities, they fall into this category.

4. **Overwhelm**: Next is our mindset. The thoughts and emotions that we feel day to day, especially those we see as negative. Overwhelm can covers a host of other emotions like tired, stuck, insecure, doubtful, hurt, frustrated, unclear, and more. It's sometimes the only word we know to describe how we feel.

5. **Self care/Spouse**: How we care for ourselves establishes the foundation for every other part of our family's life, including our relationship with our spouse. We as women tend to neglect taking care of ourselves so significantly that we hurt our health and our marriages. Let us infuse our core values into our lives so deeply that we make sure to care for our own needs and keep our marriage a high priority. This means our needs and our spouses' needs receive the time, attention, and value they each deserve.

When we take the first letter of each of the key words above and put them together, they form the acronym C.H.A.O.S. When life gets busy, one of these 5 areas needs our attention.

When life feels like a mess, ask:

- Which one of these areas is calling out for my attention right now?
- How can I intentionally manage that area right now?
- How can I use my core values to turn things around and create a practical solution?

EPILOGUE

Intentional parenting is for families who desire to live a life of purpose and meaning in spite of living in a busy, noisy, and chaotic world. Everyday they are choosing to live according to their God-given purpose and to resist the tempting distractions. My hope is that this book has in-spired all of us to become more intentional. This is more than just a daily goal that we check off our to-do list, but my hope is that this becomes our deepest heart-level commitment.

Most parenting advice centers around how-to information for raising kids and building a successful family. Parenting styles are burdensome attempts to guarantee that we raise our children the 'right' way. The truth is what we do as parents, is not nearly as important as who we become as we parent. In our efforts to avoid making mistakes and potentially messing up our kids' we get ourselves all tangled up in endless styles and tech-niques.

We so desperately want the promises they claim though.
- Easy parenting? Yes.
- Obedient children? Yes.

The promises are good enough to get us to buy the book and attend the conference. After all, from day one we have wished for an owner's manual to help us care for the overwhelming needs of our children. Our desperation for a solution leaves us vulnerable.

But if what we are trying to escape is the very thing that we need? What if the parenting challenges we face are part of a bigger plan?

That is exactly what is happening. The issues and the challenges are not happening to us, they're happening for us. They are exactly what we need. God has a plan.

Here's the truth. Our days are numbered. James 4:14 says- "You are a mist that appears for a little while and then vanishes" It's easy to forget this when our minds are distracted. But there's hope. Even though tomorrow isn't promised to any of us, we have today. We have right now. This moment.

If a child lives at home until age 18 – that's a total of 6,570 days.
If they are 5 years old 1,825 of those days have passed.
If they are 10 years old 3,650 of those days have passed.

No matter how old our children are or how young, today is a good day to refocus and live on purpose.

Seize this moment and rise above the noise and distractions. Allow the Spirit of God to cleanse our hearts and minds of all untruths, subtle lies, and myths. Now is the time to be intentional and full of purpose. Tomorrow may be too late.

What is it we want our children to know?
What do we want them to understand?

Set our hearts and minds on making that our highest priority. Focus on what really matters. Resist the urge to look to the left or the right or try yet another parenting style. Follow the path that God has set. Pursue the path of purpose.

Visit SusanSeay.com – for more information and resources to support you.

How can I help you or the parents in your community?

Please don't hesitate to let me know how I can serve you.

Let's be intentional parents together!

Core Values List

Abundance	Efficiency	Improvement
Accountable	Equality	Independence
Adventurous	Excellence	Individuality
Balance	Exploration	Initiative
Beauty	Fairness	Inner Peace
Challenge	Faith	Innovation
Clarity	Faithfulness	Integrity
Cleanliness	Flexibility	Intelligence
Commitment	Forgiveness	Intuition
Communica-	Freedom	Joy
tion	Friendship	Justice
Community	Frugality	Knowledge
Compassion	Fulfillment	Leadership
Concern	Fun	Learning
Confidence	Generosity	Love
Connection	Genuineness	Loyalty
Contentment	Goodwill	Meaning
Cooperation	Goodness	Merit
Creativity	Gratitude	Modesty
Decisiveness	Hard Work	Nurturing
Determina-	Harmony	Obedience
tion	Healing	Openness
Discipline	Health	Optimism
Diversity	Honesty	Patriotism
Education	Honor	Peace

Perseverance	Prosperity	Tradition
Persistence	Punctuality	Tranquility
Personal	Purpose	Trust
Growth	Strength	Truth
Practicality	Success	Unity
Privacy	Systems	Wealth
Problem	Thinking	Wisdom
Solving	Teamwork	
Professional-	Timeliness	
ism	Tolerance	

ABOUT THE AUTHOR

Powerful, practical wisdom is what you'll find with Susan Seay. After her many years of study to include a Bachelor of Arts degree in Psychology from Texas State University, Susan loves to look for patterns for successfully raising a family, so that she can share her findings with others. Moms and families across the globe connect with her through podcast interviews, speaking and her facilitating, as well as private mentoring and coaching sessions. She and her husband Ron are actively parenting their own 7 children in Austin, Texas.

Visit: SusanSeay.c

Questions Intentional Parents Ask Their Kids – card set

24 cards containing over 44 questions

Including:

* 10 questions to ask your children every year
* 10 great questions to ask to keep the conversation going
* 5 questions to ask when your kids won't listen

Super Simple Ways to Build A Rock Solid Relationship with Your Kids - card set - 27 cards

Made with busy parents in mind.

You can build a strong connection with your children, in even when your schedule gets busy. Long to-do lists don't have to get in the way of you having an amazing relationship with your kids.

Order both sets today for just $25 + S/H
Go to **SusanSeay.com/shop** for these and other resources.